Nature's Nuptials

Melinda Jane
Nature's Nuptials

Nature's Nuptials
ISBN 978 1 76041 772 7
Copyright © text Melinda Jane 2019
The Poet Mj (www.thepoetmj.com)
Cover painting: Hamish MacDonald (www.locostudio.com.au)

First published 2019 by
GINNINDERRA PRESS
PO Box 3461 Port Adelaide 5015
www.ginninderrapress.com.au

Contents

Your Sea	7
Briefly Butterfly	8
Cat	9
Apricot Jam	10
Rain	12
Veranda Art	13
Common Froglet	14
The Birds in Me	15
The Race	17
Sea Dance	20
Full Moon	21
A kaleidoscope, flutter, swarm of butterflies	22
Serpentine	23
Riverbend	24
Memoirs of a Diary	26
Camouflaged	30
Bowing Waves	31
The She-oaks Bend	32
Schubert Impromptu No 3 Piano Played On	35
River Water in the Veins	36
Nature	37
Obsession	38
Screens	40
Deciduous	43

Your Sea

The wilderness
of your belly
I stop there
I cannot trespass
your vastness
your opened mouth
and rushing tongue
Your voice
Your salty
sea kisses
Your vertically
shooting
starry straights
north to your
milky way
At your water's edge
I see not
your depth
'Sultry Temptress'
You sing me in
to swim
drown within
your lapping arms
and legs
to my watery rest.

Briefly Butterfly

Briefly butterfly flies by
time escapes, flitter, flutter
passes by, lilting monolith
caressed messages
tattooed upon wings.

Cat

Cat purred and scratched
all at once
with those sharp yellowing eyes
menacing with glee
watching to see if person
would flinch, claws needing
the pin cushion lap.

Soft material
pricks of flesh
all the while hypnotising
person with rhythmic purrs
and sweet winks
devouring eyes.

The sadistic pleasure of Cat
torturing prey
settling down
on warm bonnet
of person's lap
as only Cat could do.

Apricot Jam

Opening their blouse,
slicing into their souls,
knifing their hearts out.

The smell of one and a half kilograms of
fleshed, ripe permeating
gardens, after a thunderstorm,
folded in granules of ant-like sugar grains,
with a hint, tinged nose of cut grass, vanilla pods,
its seeds exposed like honeycomb.

A stray seed left after a shower of bitter lemon spit,
in a tizzy tongue tang of tart flavours,
ambrosial flower scents hung like fuchsias
cascading in the air.

The impregnated spice of lemon, sugar, vanilla, apricots,
overdoses on sparkling summer white wine in tropical heat.

The flick of eternal flame, scorching their backs,
the nest of bubbles, burping through,
this imagined brew,
coughing up potions for love makers,
apricots surfing, syrupy waves.

Twenty-five minutes of hot effervescence
the home pungent with tropical fruit infusions.

The eternal flame mute and let
the tart liquid of golden oil
cough, splutter and taper off.

Abated heat and ladled into
warmed jars for God's future feasts.
Christmas plum pudding with blood jam,
scones on a cold winter night with fatting cream,
choked in rubble yellow from the past sun,
or ice cream coated with a film of this magic brew
to sweeten and tang the pallet
with creamy, vanilla ice cream in spring.

All year round
the textured gravel
baked on toast,
ritual after ritual, bathed in morning light,
dawn comes with percolating coffee steam
and apricot jam,
smeared on broken toast.

Rain

It rained till its heart poured out.
Sobbing like a lost child.
Nothing could shelter from its pain.

It gave up its emotions,
feeling unguarded,
a divorcing season.

Veranda Art

Previous owners forsaken art
Picasso blue, Pollock splashes.
Sea daisies dapple each crack.
Snails trail their lined abstractions.
Surfaces flourish in a Monet impression.

Jittering, merry blue wrens
prance like Bangarra dance company.
Magpies lyrical ambience gives rise
to Brahms concertos, while an opera of
kookaburras parade on stage lines.

Surrealism comes from the frog's leaps.
Naturalism painted grass, nature's aspect.
Cubism from the metal grate, screen door print.
The stilled life, the portrait of a woman
standing there, by the arch way.

Common Froglet

I spy
a froglet
identified
the 'common froglet'.

But froglet
not common or plain
richly spotted, forest browns
fondly small.

Perched
above the hemline
sunning, baking on
lilting lily leaf.

Impressed
upon my mind
I christened froglet
'Herbert Rebert'.

The Birds in Me

My grey strike-thrush time,
grey, calling out behind
the green leafy blinds
you may hear me but not see me.

When I am Poet Mj
in a dashing splash of blues,
a blue wren on stage
calling out my poems of rhyme.

Then I am meditating, my soul and
mind have ascended to the sky
I the wedge-tailed eagle spying out my prey,
plunging I clasp my meal, I feast.

Settling in with Beloved,
I become the tawny frogmouth,
sitting on the gum limb,
watching for the frogs
so I can gorge till dawn.

Sometimes I am nasty,
a New Holland honeyeater
bombarding those who dare come into my terrain.
Incessant chirping I am the non-native sparrow.
Other days I hang out with my friends,
on the electrical lines,
laughing like kookaburras.

Then when life stressors become
too much, I become the nightly
mopoke owl, I weep, cry out
mournfully in my needs
and longings unfulfilled

                                      All the birds in me

The Race

Whip up hooves
Whip up nerves
In the fray
Cluttered together
Thud, gallop speed
Jounce thighs stampede
Nostrils flare
Electric sinews fire
Pulsating hooves
Radiating bodies
Buff the curving rail
Steel and nails
The clustered platoon
Thronged harpoon
Heat
Compete
That buzz hum
The race
The slew
They flew
Rubbing rubble
Grind tumble
The forward force
The primal fear
Taut, tense pack
Last picked off track
Cunning
Stay in bustle
Tenuous steeds
Holding steady

Now on the straight
Flex forward
Heads tucked
Rock back and forth
Flow as one
Jockeys perched
Steed ruddy grace
Puff of engine steam
Cheers cultivate a lift
Jockeys stub whips
Finely wired skin
Froth like icing on a cake
Soaked back
Running sweat, neck, forelocks
Salted brow
One stream flowing
In a river of thoroughbreds
Separate swift
The herd drifts
Hung, cling rump, wither
Release winner
Stretch neck
Mare with flecks
Bridle, breastplate
Pinched tongue liberate
Full throttle
Jostle
Past the invisible line
Then lollop strides

To jog steam
Perfection engine teem
All knotted spring
Wired piston rings
Sodden jocks
With mud, dust, grit
Escapes to mindful watchfulness
Guarding horses artfulness
Fright or fight
Held apart
Grasping
Clip on leads
Steering steeds
Herd in triumph ticks
Chaotic sounds
Cheers all around
The race.

Sea Dance

Scattered jewels
hemming your skirt line
lace froth of taffeta
dancing ballerina
flow, twirl
twirl, flow
dancing in taffeta green.

Ballerina,
serenade the swimmers
with theatrics
swirls, twirls and leaps
dancing within taffeta green.

Full Moon

I see you there,
like my own child.
Raised high above
my shoulders, carelessly
tossed in triumph
high above my arms.

I see you there,
like my own child.
Full and laughter rich.
Bold, milky and round.
I see you there,
like my own child
full moon night.

A kaleidoscope, flutter, swarm of butterflies

A kaleidoscope, flutter, swarm of butterflies
flew, blew this way and that
colours in flurry, hurry skywards
prayers of flutter, lighted, caressed aura
rainbow wings, flecked illumination
ruminating thoughts on air.

Serpentine

The stirring belly
Serpent restless
Bulrushes move
Frenzy frog
Simmer
Left bathers
Rippling currents
Flows S-shape dance.

Course the passage
Cross
Twisted climb
Hibernation
Fold sculptured tongue
Summer retold
Simmer deception.

Riverbend

Clift's personality shadows
tight rows of shanties
clinging like plastic wrap
pish posh, pish posh
lungs grapple their polls
model boy whose body gleams so sheen
lapping ripples
from his jet stream
smell of pond beer
abbreviated jetty
fishing lines
draped necklaces
fish tailings, scales
smell diesel
scrimpy dory chokes past
brave
halfway out
bobbing heads, taste like beans
canned in river sauce
bending round
sun lotion beauties
glamming on show boats
with jet skis
and older couple
selfie canoe snap.

This poet's desire
to cross, this
godless land
over
clamber to
virgin
smelling Aboriginal habitation
smoke, eucalyptus leaves, crushed reeds
woven baskets
bark canoes
fish, mussels from downstream
communal meal
then
zip, zip, zoom…
pissy, modern sound
river drowned.

Memoirs of a Diary

Chapter 1

The snowdrop kissed the diary
caressed the organising creed
one pure, colourless silk
fluttered, flittered, filtered time
increments, incense of things
scattered to universal dust
this precious time, challenging
lines of lineation
web spindles of fine threads
memories
invisibly hung, spinning.

Chapter 2

A web
to do list today
priorities
properly propelled
ordered, orderly, orders
call, claim, purchase
reply, reply, reply
forward
attention to
reply.

Chapter 3

The forest memoirs
the web's alleys, lanes looping
spiders hungry traffic and
the silent bed of moss
hidden fungus, lingering on logs
pine needles pointing and
paths of snails crossing intersections, under
cool, coils of fanned canopy
which whisper calmly
while wispy light
chorus under cathedrals
of banners
cloistered in praise.

Chapter 4

Twisted twister
modern memoirs
The forest grey looms
lions prowl
pearl lines sweep
high jutting skyscrapers
peddling, padding structures
scattered underneath
the scraper's shadowy canopies
with minions snails scrambling
webs, emails
reply, reply, reply
forward
to an organised state
cloistered minds
shift, shuffle, lurching forward
towards the spider's web.

Camouflaged

The encounter arrives
exposed on the coral road
little leaf grasshopper
jumping salty
popping like a green chili pepper
boom, ba-bam, hopper dash
boom, ba-bam, agile stunt
light caramel, flecks of leafy green
camouflaged, like me.

Flick, jumping salty
you intimate
steps of a tango dance
my counter-action
a light samba
then
salty jumper
sprightly gone
into verdure
camouflaged, like me.

Bowing Waves

Sand in my teeth,
grit between my toes,
waves bowing down
a pray at a time
in submission to their deity
up there in the sky.

Farewell to my soul,
it passed me by,
I ended up there;
a star in the sky.

The She-oaks Bend

The she-oaks bend
liked gnarled, aged backs,
crooked, black faces stained
ravished by fires laid.

To stand among death
now on this peak,
peek out forward
towards the ruins
gulped by fire and ash.

The spire
summer residence
of vice-regals past,
the castle consumed by fire,
like casting a rune.

To my back I sight
sighing she-oak stumps
with copper wings, they
moan of days past, when
all was virgin blessed.

Glinting eyes right
I capture only
land, without hands of little deities
to mess up and mill around in.

I telescope the view,
this dragon's mount,
my eyes now descend
to a goat track, where
a silhouetted, solitary car
presses into the mountain's base
and now crawls home.

Perched far below to left's eyes
a little creek meanders
silently where noon gums
shagged with crystal blue
moss and child-ferns grow.

I fondly played in that creek,
heard its garbled laughter, as it
floated over slime and pebbles.

I cupped my hands under tadpoles,
those polliwogs
with foaming legs, sprouting tails
transforming from childhood into adolescence.

Then upwards glance
the moon shines
in afternoon jest, it says
'Surprise!'

Turn then, tread,
tracking back down the incline,
scuttle over bronze rocks,
shuffle over dying arms
tearing at my garments,
now left in their undergrowth,
a testament that I was once there
staring out, perched on this mountain top.

Schubert Impromptu No 3 Piano Played On

It was like the hands were liquefied,
running over the blacks and whites,
whites and blacks, forward on into infinity,
as it wafted, floated incandescently wi-fi
through my home, my bones, sinews vibrated
like the strumming of a cello or
like a slow dancing willow against the wind.

Then I plunged with it like a mermaid,
into the sea depths, like fingers touching the keys
with a measured rational emotion, then
flung like petals carelessly to the ground
and then as the eagle picks up and soars,
on currents, invisible to my eyes –
Schubert Impromptu No 3 piano played on.

River Water in the Veins

Salt on the tongue and
river water in the veins.
Songs of reed concerto movements
in G major.
High blue cathedral skies
roofed in by woollen cloth.

Skyline free of humanity's claws,
those jagged, grey edges.
This quiet edge of existence,
tempered with the call to the waters.
A religious conversion
back to nature.
Salt on the tongue and
river water in the veins.

Nature

I wish to hold the passion of a wild steed in gallop.

The hard working burdens of the plough
as I, Clydesdale toil.

Grant me the heart of the police horse,
peace commands standing
rabble rebels
with or without cause.

Pull up steady pony in harness
know when Fate takes the reins
and Master does not.

Farrier, trim my hooves, and
discard the clippings.

Grant me the strength, to hold fast
in a meadow under storm.
And store clover to fatten my rump
when bitter waits of winter fall.

Horse I be
Knoweth Lord

Obsession

Holding you
creeps me, like
a slippery fish
with scales.

Your green top
a tutu or a wig.
The touch, Braille.

Always there
in the sauntering heat, of
cricket, tennis division
sweating under the
glazing sun.

I like it
when you are
wretchedly ripe.

Cheery
diseased designed
with chickenpox.

Delicately
I hold your
emerald tutu
dance, waltz you
into my mouth.

Death burst
tart, my eyes wink
then sweet addiction runs
along my system.

I re-imagine
consuming you
again.

My addiction for you
is consummated
in many ways
smeared on buttery toast
held, surfing on cream
a meringue, or
whipped to a frenzy
blended in a cheesecake
just naked, raw
tobogganing down a slope
of vanilla ice cream.

This Braille
written on your breast
codes out the word
'strawberry'.

Screens

start with classical music
tune your mind towards this
and the sky
when moods are high
swing with the jazz
and reach for the waves

start with this poem
and bite
and bite
then chew till
it infests your insides
insidious disease

pull up ten miles from work
and walk all the way
no iPhone screen to ponder
but the scream of light
steps eyes on architecture screens
man-made and god likes

pull away from the curve
of toxic relationships
and shed a hair at a time
and find less is more

shuttle yourself
to a podcast
and cast away to new horizons
your imaging schemes
and tie down only
your moods and your escape
from this rhythmic transport hub

start with a sugarless drink
of H two O and
gulp back toes that
waltz with the dog
down to the beach, park, street

beat to
step to
start to
breathe
one spot
on the view
and think waves
flow while
breath molecules
flow

start with
smaller sways of screens
and sway away to aeroplane mode
for half your day
and see
see
in the mirror
of the faces that acknowledge you
and glow

turn then
greet
the sun
turn
bow
greet the earth
turn towards
our faces
and heart screens

Deciduous

It's like coral
branching up
under the sea
crystal sky.

It's like an ending, of
a wedding
glories music streams
forth, as guests
shower the couple
with confetti.

It's like a dot painting
the hills, the water holes
the sacred places
a map of their dreamtimes
in ochre, khaki, amber
dotted on spots
lines, rivers a story.

It's like a choir
dropping sonorous notes
on the air, flowing
drifting towards the edge, of
the stage, rehearsals
go on, angelic lilts float
in yellow tones of sun.

It's like henna
ritually painted on
feet, Orissi Dancer
curling symbols
like the leaves
and branches in
wind, temple ceremony
jangle bells, jewelled
decorations on her.

It's like my hair
changing seasons, colours
salt and pepper, greys
shine like bark, under
the tones of lighter shades
the letting go, leaves
shedding hairs, autumn leaves
ageing, this apple tree
it's like the souls, I'm gathering
towards.

www.ingramcontent.com/pod-product-compliance
Lightning Source LLC
Chambersburg PA
CBHW062206100526
44589CB00014B/1980